Clara Barton: The Life and Legacy of the Civil War Nurse Who Founded the American Red Cross

By Charles River Editors

About Charles River Editors

Charles River Editors is a boutique digital publishing company, specializing in bringing history back to life with educational and engaging books on a wide range of topics. Keep up to date with our new and free offerings with this 5 second sign up on our weekly mailing list, and visit Our Kindle Author Page to see other recently published Kindle titles.

We make these books for you and always want to know our readers' opinions, so we encourage you to leave reviews and look forward to publishing new and exciting titles each week.

Introduction

"I may be compelled to face danger, but never fear it, and while our soldiers can stand and fight, I can stand and feed and nurse them." – Clara Barton

The Civil War was the deadliest conflict in American history, and had the two sides realized it would take 4 years and inflict over a million casualties, it might not have been fought. Since it did, however, Americans have long been fascinated by the Civil War, marveling at the size of the battles, the leadership of the generals, and the courage of the soldiers. For over 150 years, the war has been subjected to endless debate among civilians, historians, and the generals themselves.

The Civil War is often considered one of the first modern wars, and while technology affected what happened on the battlefield, technology and new methods also improved the way soldiers were cared for away from the front lines. Civil War medicine is understandably (and rightly) considered primitive by 21st century standards, but the ways in which injured and sick soldiers were removed behind the lines and nursed were considered state-of-the-art in the 1860s, and nobody was more responsible for that than Clara Barton, the "Florence Nightingale of America."

Barton had been an educator and clerk before the Civil War broke out in 1861, but almost immediately, she went to work attempting to nurse injured Union soldiers and ensure army hospitals were properly supplied. By 1862, she was shadowing Union armies near Washington to bring supplies, clean field hospitals, and directly nurse wounded soldiers herself. In short order, she was recognized as the "Angel of the Battlefield."

In the wake of the war, she gave speeches about her experiences and even went abroad to serve in a similar capacity during the Franco-Prussian War, and eventually she brought back the tenets of the International Red Cross to found the American Red Cross. Under her leadership, the organization would assist not just during wars, but also during natural disasters and other humanitarian crises, roles that the American Red Cross continues to fulfill today.

Clara Barton: The Life and Legacy of the Civil War Nurse Who Founded the American Red Cross chronicles her remarkable life, and the manner in which she changed nursing in America forever. Along with pictures depicting important people, places, and events, you will learn about Clara Barton like never before.

Clara Barton: The Life and Legacy of the Civil War Nurse Who Founded the American Red Cross

About Charles River Editors

Introduction

    Clara's Early Years

    A First

    The Civil War

    A Celebrity at Home and Abroad

    The American Red Cross

    Online Resources

    Further Reading

Free Books by Charles River Editors

Discounted Books by Charles River Editors

Clara's Early Years

"The patriot blood of my father was warm in my veins." – Clara Barton

Clarissa Harlowe Barton was born on Christmas Day, 1821, in North Oxford, Massachusetts. She was a later-life child, 10 years younger than the youngest of her two brothers and two sisters. Her father, Captain Stephen Barton, was prominent in local politics as a selectman for the town and as part of the local militia. As such, he fought against Native American tribes in northwest Massachusetts, as part of the unit headed by General Anthony Wayne. He and his wife, Sarah, were also active members in New England' burgeoning Progressive movement.

Captain Barton took great pride in his family's background of service to the nation and sought to inspire his children to continue in that tradition. He also emphasized the importance of early and thorough education for both his sons and daughters, so much so that the family sent Clara to school at the age of three.

Stephen Barton

Sarah Barton

School was something of a trial for one so much younger than the others, and Clara's shyness made her classroom life even more difficult. Eventually, she made one close friend, Nancy Fitts, whom she later called the "playmate of my childhood; the 'chum' of laughing girlhood; the faithful, trusted companion of young womanhood, and the beloved life friend that the relentless grasp of time has neither changed, nor taken from me."

Outside of school, around those she knew and trusted, Barton was full of life and vigor. In fact, her parents, especially her mother, were concerned that she had too much energy, and they only worried more when the family moved to the Learned farmstead to help Clara's cousin's widow survive without her husband. In her biography, *Clara Barton, Professional Angel*, Elizabeth Brown Pryor explained, "The Learneds were allowed to stay on, but Clara's family also moved into the house. The Learned boys, Jerry and Otis, and their friend Lovett Simpson, became her firm friends...It was a time of revelations and a burst of freedom for Clara. She was away from the watchful eyes of six surrogate parents…She idolized Otis and Jerry, and they admired her extravagantly, for she 'could run as fast and ride better' than they."

Though they were Progressives, young Clara's parents were still products of the late 18th century and thus did not approve of her antics. Pryor noted, "It was perhaps inevitable that Clara's long tether would eventually be pulled in, especially when the benign neglect afforded her by her parents had had some unfortunate repercussions…her parents began to question the appropriateness of the little girl's tomboy ways. Her father forbade her to learn to skate, something her male companions enjoyed tremendously. Undaunted, she slipped out at night, tempted by the smooth glare ice and bright stars."

Her efforts nearly ended in tragedy. Clara later recalled, "Swifter and swifter we went, until at length we reached a spot where the ice had been cracked and was full of sharp edges. These threw me and the speed with which we were progressing…gave terrific opportunity for cuts and wounded knees." The young girl had to explain her injuries to her parents and admitted that, for a time, she "despised herself and failed to sleep or eat."

Clara got her first nursing experience when she was only 10 after her older brother David was injured in a fall. Though it was initially assumed he was fine, he began suffering headaches and fever, so the family doctor, in keeping with a common practice of the time, bled him repeatedly and blistered his skin. As was often the case, those "treatments" did not prove to be good remedies, and as David continued to suffered, Clara took upon herself the role of nurse. She later explained that "from the first days and nights of illness, I remained near his side. The fever ran on and over all the traditional turning points, seven, fourteen, twenty-one days. I could not be taken away from him except by compulsion, and he was unhappy until my return. I learned to take all directions for his medicines from his physician (who had eminent counsel) and to administer them like a genuine nurse…My little hands became schooled to the handling of the great, loathsome, crawling leeches which were at first so many snakes to me, and no fingers could so painlessly dress the angry blisters; and thus it came about, that I was the accepted and acknowledged nurse of a man almost too ill to recover. Finally, as the summer passed, the fever gave way, and for a wonder the patient did not...Late in the autumn he stood on his feet for the first time since July. Still sleepless, nervous, cold, dyspeptic — a mere wreck of his former self...I realize now how carefully and apprehensively the whole family watched the little nurse, but I had no idea of it then. I thought my position the most natural thing in the world; I almost forgot that there was an outside to the house."

Despite her efforts, her brother continued to struggle with medical problems, until the family finally tried something new. According to Clara, "This state of things continued with little change…for two years, when, entirely unexpected, the most tabooed and little known of all medical treatments, restored him to health...The result was the removal of the patient to the home asylum of the doctor for treatment. In three weeks he was so far restored as to return home and take his place in his business, like one come back from the dead..."

Barton never explained what this mysterious treatment was, but once her brother was healthy again, her life went back to normal. Perhaps inevitably, she quickly missed the joy and sense of importance she had found in nursing: "This singular mode of life, at so young an age, could not have been without its characteristic effects. In some respects it had served to heighten serious defects. The seclusion had increased the troublesome bashfulness. I had grown even more timid, shrinking and sensitive in the presence of others; absurdly careful and methodical for a child; afraid of giving trouble by letting my wants be known, thereby giving the very pain I sought to avoid, and instead of feeling that my freedom gave me time for recreation or play, it seemed to me like time wasted, and I looked anxiously about for some useful occupation."

Feeling perhaps that being isolated from her peers for so long may have caused Barton to become even more introverted, her parents decided to send her away to school. She remembered that "it was decided that I be sent to Col. Stone's High school, to board in his family and go home occasionally. This arrangement, I learned in later years, had a double object. I was what is known as a bashful child, timid in the presence of other persons, a condition of things found impossible to correct at home. In the hope of overcoming this undesirable mauvaise honte, it was decided to throw me among strangers...The house and school rooms adjoined, and seemed enormously large. The household was also large. The long family table with the…preceptor, my loved and feared teacher at three years, at its head, seemed to me something formidable. There were probably one hundred and fifty pupils daily in the ample school rooms, of which I was perhaps the youngest, except the colonel's own children."

The school proved to be less than helpful when it came to making Barton less shy. She admitted, "My studies were chosen with great care. I remember among them, ancient history with charts. The lessons were learned to repeat by rote. I found difficulty both in learning the proper names and in pronouncing them, as I had not quite outgrown my lisp...I am not sure that I was really homesick, but the days seemed very long, especially Sundays. I was in constant dread of doing something wrong…My studies gave me no trouble, but I grew very tired, felt hungry all the time but dared not eat, grew thin and pale…finally at the end of the term a consultation was held between the colonel, my father and our beloved family physician…and it was decided to take me home until a little older, and wiser, I could hope...If I ever could have gotten entirely over [my timid sensitiveness], it would have given far less annoyance and trouble to myself all through life.

While Barton was comfortable around those she knew well, she remained extremely shy when it came to interacting with those outside her family. Both of her older sisters were schoolteachers, and the family suggested that she take on this profession, too, again hoping that being in front of children who had to obey her would help her become more comfortable with people of all ages.

Since she had received an excellent education, Clara had no problem passing the teacher's exam in 1839, months before her 18th birthday. She had always enjoyed studying, and she looked forward to sharing what she had learned with her charges, so the way was set for her success. Even discipline came easily. One of her students later wrote to her, "I remember you walking about with your ruler in your hand...I don't remember that you ever punished anyone, you used your ruler for other purposes."

Barton's success at her first school led those in charge to give her a larger school in a nearby community. There, her hopes to keep control of her students by relying on affection were dashed when several unruly boys refused to do as they were told. Accustomed to the ways of teenaged men, Barton wasted no time taking action, as Pryor related: "One morning, when the most troublesome boy swaggered tardily into the classroom, annoying the pupils and mocking Barton…she took action. She requested him to come forward, and as he walked saucily up the aisle, she pulled a long riding whip from her desk, lashing out and tripping him while the other pupils watched with horror. Barton continued to wield the whip, jerking him to his knees until he apologized to the school for his actions. She then dismissed the shaken students for the day and suggested that they have a picnic in the meadow near the school." This proved to be a defining moment for Barton in her teaching career, and she noted, "I had learnt what discipline meant, and it was for all time as far as that school was concerned; none ever needed more than a kindly smile."

At the same time, Barton was ambitious, so much so that men in her era considered her unusually and overly ambitious for a woman of her time. Undaunted, she aimed to move forward, and she was not satisfied with merely teaching. Her biographer Pryor explained, "The control Barton exercised over this school further enhanced her reputation…for nearly ten years her services were actively sought in both Oxford and the surrounding area. Rarely did she teach the same school twice…It intrigued her to ferret out the unique problems of each schoolhouse and to channel her pupils' energies into study instead of mischief. But once the problems were conquered and the school settled down to a contented routine, Clara's active mind became distracted…She was pleased, therefore, when the school board in Oxford requested that she teach the winter term of a particularly difficult school."

Barton almost never taught at that school, for the board insisted that she only be paid what women were paid for summer work instead of the full salary. Showing her mettle, Barton turned down the position, insisting, "I may sometimes be willing to teach for nothing, but if paid at all, I shall never do a man's work for less than a man's pay." After being impressed by her work, the board ultimately acquiesced to her demands. It also made use of her talents by sending her to steadily more challenging schools. These early experiences not only helped her overcome her shyness, but gave her a chance to hone her administrative and political skills.

Those would soon come quite in handy.

A First

An 1851 portrait of Barton

"I have an almost complete disregard of precedent, and a faith in the possibility of something better. It irritates me to be told how things have always been done. I defy the tyranny of precedent. I go for anything new that might improve the past." – Clara Barton

Barton taught for 12 years until her mother's death in 1851. With his wife gone and all his children pursuing their own lives, Captain Barton chose to close up the family's home at this time and move into smaller bachelor quarters. At a loss for something to do, and bored with teaching, Clara decided to further her education by enrolling in the Clinton Liberal Institute in Clinton, New York. Established in 1831 by the Universalist Church, the Institute existed "not only for general purposes of science and literature, but with a particular view of furnishing with an education young men designed for the ministry of reconciliation." The time at Clinton proved helpful for Barton, as she made new friends and got to sharpen her mind with lively discussions with other men and women. In fact, she was such an outstanding student that the school's principal took particular notice of her, and the two eventually became romantically involved.

As that suggests, Barton was involved with a number of men during her lifetime, and though she never married, her nephew, Stephen E. Barton, provided an appropriate reason why she never did: "My aunt said to me one time that I must not think she had never known any experience of love. She said that she had had her romances and love affairs like other girls; but that in her young womanhood, though she thought of different men as possible lovers, no one of them measured up to her ideal of a husband. She said to me that she could think of herself with satisfaction as a wife and mother, but that on the whole she felt that she had been more useful to the world by being free from matrimonial ties."

Barton remained at Clinton only a short time before returning to teaching, this time in Hightstown, New Jersey. While there, she heard worrisome stories about the condition of the schools in nearby Bordentown. David Henry Burton, who authored *Clara Barton: in the service of humanity*, explained, "She journeyed to Trenton, the state capital, to suggest to education authorities there was a real need for public education free of cost to the students...Getting no encouragement from Trenton, Barton returned to Bordentown with an 'idea.' Why not found a free school? It was a daring thought, daring enough to fire her spirit and throw her energy into high gear."

Calling upon the skills of persuasion she had honed in the past, as well as on her brother Stephen for help, Clara convinced the school board to authorize a new school, and she offered to teach without a salary if the board would pay for a building, desks, and other supplies. According to Burton, "Her purpose was not to demonstrate her personal devotion to education but the genuine advantages the town would experience by having a non-fee-paying school...The school was soon brimming with eager students. A friend, Fanny Childs, came from Oxford to assist Clara with the teaching. Her free school idea was a complete success, and the town responded by building a fine new building to house classes, turning dream into reality."

Unfortunately, disappointment lay just around the corner. Burton continued, "Clara was stunned then when the school board insisted that a man be appointed headmaster because they determined an enterprise that included over six hundred boys and girls was simply beyond…a woman, and so young a woman at that. Barton took unkindly to her denomination--it was really a demotion--as 'female assistant' and was further angered to learn that J. Kirby Burnham, the head, was paid $500 while she was to receive only $250." Furious, she and Childs both resigned and left the school and the town.

Looking for a new challenge and perhaps a bit of adventure, Barton moved in 1855 to Washington, D.C., where she took a job as a clerk in the US Patent Office. She was the first woman to ever hold such a clerkship, though she was quickly "demoted" to being a copyist. Burton described her experience: "She was paid at a rate of ten cents per one hundred words copied, a task at which Clara grew remarkably skillful and from which she learned a great deal about the state of developing technology in a variety of fields...she earned on average about eighty dollars per month, a sum sufficient to live in modest comfort. Her carefully scripted writing style and the rigorous honesty displayed in her work soon made Clara virtually indispensable...The employment of Barton and several other female copyists at the Patent Office was by no means the standard arrangement...[Patent Office Head Charles] Mason was one of the few superintendents who was willing to hire women, even sparingly...His chief, Robert McClelland, secretary of interior, was of a different mind...He wrote…: 'there is such an obvious impropriety in the mixing of the sexes within the walls of a public office that I am determined to arrest the process.' In Barton's behalf Mason resisted this attempt to deny him his most trusted subordinate...for the next year and a half she was paid at an annual rate of $1,400. By the standards of the day this was a goodly sum, Mason's salary being only $3,000."

Unfortunately, it was politics more than sexism that eventually cost Barton her job, for when Democrat James Buchanan came into office in 1856, Barton and many other "Black Republicans" lost their jobs. With no other government work available to her, Barton returned home in 1857 and remained there until just before the Civil War broke out, at which time she returned to Washington and took a job again as a copyist.

The Civil War

"This conflict is one thing I've been waiting for. I'm well and strong and young - young enough to go to the front. If I can't be a soldier, I'll help soldiers." – Clara Barton

Though it is common knowledge that the first shots of the Civil War were fired at Fort Sumter in Charleston, South Carolina, the shots fired did not hit anyone. Though there were casualties during the surrender ceremony, ironically, the first blood was shed in anger occurred during the Baltimore Riot on April 19, 1861, when militia members from Massachusetts and Pennsylvania making their way to Washington were attacked by Confederate sympathizers. The injured Massachusetts men were sent ahead to Washington to recuperate, and when Barton heard that they were coming into town, she met the train at the station and began organizing nursing and other services for the 40 men as they arrived. She then accompanied them to the Capitol Building, at that time still an unfinished shell, where they were to be treated. Using her Massachusetts connections, she appealed to the civilians back home to send clothing, bandages, and food to Washington, where she personally saw to it that the men received the best care she could provide. She also recruited other women to help with her efforts.

A picture of Lincoln's 1861 inauguration outside the unfinished Capitol

A contemporary depiction of the Baltimore Riot of 1861

In the months that followed, Barton threw herself into working on behalf of the Union soldiers. She consulted with doctors who, overworked and understaffed, recognized that she already had some nursing experience and instructed her on the best ways to acquire, store, and administer the few medications available at that point in time. She also recognized the importance of hope in recovery and kept the men's spirits up by reading aloud to them and engaging those strong enough in conversation. She helped write hundreds of letters home to families for sick and injured soldiers, informing worried relatives about the health and welfare of their loved ones.

Using the lobbying skills she had honed while building up schools, Barton also constantly wrote letters home asking for supplies for the wounded men at the front. By the time the fighting around Washington and Richmond reached a much larger scale in the spring of 1862, she had convinced local Ladies' Aid societies to devote themselves to rolling bandages, preparing food, and making clothing that they would then send to her in Washington, from where she distributed them to hospitals.

Though many doctors were initially dubious about her efforts, Barton was able to use her family's political connections to form quite a supportive cadre back in Massachusetts. Among those who supported her work was Massachusetts Senator Henry Wilson, who likely used his influence to help Barton persuade Quartermaster General of the Army Daniel Rucker to allow her to take supplies to the front, beginning in August 1862. In the months that followed, she also placed ads in Massachusetts papers, requesting more supplies and then managing the massive rush of items so that they got to where they were most needed.

Wilson

Once at a battlefield, she would dress wounds, make and serve food and help organize details to clean the field hospitals. Dr. James L. Dunn, attached to the 109th Pennsylvania Volunteer Infantry, wrote to his family about Barton's assistance at the Battle of Cedar Mountain in August 1862: "The Sanitary Commission, together with three or four noble self-sacrificing women, have furnished everything that could be required. I will tell you one of these women, a Miss Barton, the daughter of Judge Barton of Boston, Mass. I first met her at the battle of Cedar Mountain, where she appeared in front of the hospital at 12 o'clock at night, with a four-mule team loaded with everything needed, and at a time when we were entirely out of dressings of every kind, she supplied us with everything; and while the shells were bursting in every direction, took her course to the hospital on pour right, where she found everything wanted again. After doing everything she could on the field, she returned to Culpepper, where she stayed dealing out shirts to the naked wounded, and preparing soup, and seeing it prepared in all the hospitals."

Throughout the war, Barton insisted not only that she could face the same danger as the men, but that she should be allowed to face it as well. She explained as much while referring to the fighting at Cedar Mountain: "When our armies fought at Cedar Mountain, I broke the shackles and went into the field. Five days and nights with three hours' sleep—a narrow escape from capture—and some days of getting the wounded into hospitals at Washington…And if you chance to feel that the positions I occupied were rough and unseemly for a woman—I can only reply that they were rough and unseemly for men."

The Battle of Cedar Mountain, which Stonewall Jackson's superior Confederate force won, was a prelude to the dramatic campaign that culminated with the Second Battle of Bull Run at the end of August 1862. Less than three months before that battle, Joseph E. Johnston's Army of Northern Virginia had been pushed back nearly all the way to Richmond by George B. McClellan's Army of the Potomac, so close that Union soldiers could see the church steeples of the Confederate capital.

After Lee succeeded the wounded Johnston, he pushed McClellan's Army of the Potomac away from Richmond and back up the Peninsula in late June, only to then swing his army north to face a second Union army, John Pope's Army of Virginia. Needing to strike out before the Army of the Potomac successfully sailed back to Washington and linked up with Pope's army, Lee daringly split his army to threaten Pope's supply lines, forcing Pope to fall back to Manassas to protect his flank and maintain his lines of communication. At the same time, it left half of Lee's army (under Stonewall Jackson) potentially exposed against the larger Union army until the other wing (under James Longstreet) linked back up. Thus, in late August 1862, the Army of Northern Virginia and the Army of Virginia found themselves fighting over nearly the exact same land the South and North fought over in the First Battle of Bull Run 13 months earlier.

When Pope's army fell back to Manassas to confront Jackson, his wing of Lee's army dug in along a railroad trench and took a defensive stance. The battle began with the Union army throwing itself at Jackson the first two days, but the concentration on Stonewall's men opened up the Union army's left flank for James Longstreet's wing, which marched 30 miles in 24 hours to reach the battlefield by the late afternoon of August 29. Lee used Longstreet's wing on August 30 to deliver a devastating flank attack before enough reinforcements from the retreating Army of the Potomac reached the field, sweeping Pope's army from Manassas and forcing the Union soldiers into yet another disorderly retreat from Manassas to Washington, D.C., a scene eerily reminiscent of the First Battle of Bull Run.

Dunn, who had encountered Barton at Cedar Mountain, also took note of her at the Second Battle of Bull Run: "[W]hile the battle was raging the fiercest on Friday, who should drive up in front of our hospital but this same woman, with her mules almost dead, having made forced marches from Washington to the army. She was again a welcomed visitor to both the wounded and the surgeons." Then, following the Battle of Chantilly a few days later, Dunn wrote that when "we had nothing but our instruments, not even a bottle of wine…the cars whistled up to the station, the first person on the platform was Miss Barton, to again supply us with bandages, brandy, wine, prepared soup, jellies, meal, and every article that could be thought of. She stayed there until the last wounded soldier was placed on the cars, then bid us good bye, and left."

In early September, convinced that the best way to defend Richmond was to divert attention to Washington, Lee had decided to invade Maryland, so he asked Confederate President Jefferson Davis for approval to do so. In conjunction with giving Lee his approval, Davis wrote a public proclamation to the Southern people and, ostensibly, the Europeans whose recognition he hoped to gain. Recognizing the political sensitivity of appearing to invade the North instead of simply defending the home front, Davis cast the decision as one of self-defense, and that there was "no design of conquest."

Today the decision to invade Maryland is remembered through the prism of Lee hoping to win a major battle in the North that would bring about European recognition of the Confederacy, potential intervention, and possible capitulation by the North, whose anti-war Democrats were picking up political momentum. However, Lee also hoped that the fighting in Maryland would relieve Virginia's resources, especially the Shenandoah Valley, which served as the state's "breadbasket". And though largely forgotten today, Lee's move was controversial among his own men. Confederate soldiers, including Lee, took up arms to defend their homes, but now they were being asked to invade a Northern state. An untold number of Confederate soldiers refused to cross the Potomac River into Maryland. With the benefit of hindsight, historians now believe that Lee's entire Army of Northern Virginia had perhaps 50,000 men at most and possibly closer to 30,000 during the Maryland campaign. It's unclear how Lee's army, which numbered 55,000 before the Maryland Campaign, suffered such a steep drop in manpower, but historians have cited a number of factors, including disease and soldiers' refusal to invade the North.

The most fateful decision of the Maryland Campaign was made almost immediately, when early on Lee decided to divide his army into four parts across Maryland. As luck would have it, Union soldiers found Lee's plans, known as the "Lost Orders," and George McClellan's Army of the Potomac quickly gave chase to try to defeat the Confederates before they could link back up. That would bring them to Sharpsburg, Maryland, where the two armies would fight along Antietam Creek.

The Battle of Antietam was the bloodiest day in American history, and it took place on the 75th anniversary of the signing of the Constitution. On September 17, 1862, nearly 25,000 would become casualties, and Lee's army would barely survive fighting the much bigger Northern army. Although the battle was tactically a draw, it resulted in forcing Lee's army out of Maryland and back into Virginia, making it a strategic victory for the North and an opportune time for President Abraham Lincoln to issue the Emancipation Proclamation, freeing all slaves in the rebellious states.

Antietam is where soldiers and generals in the Union army truly began to notice Clara Barton and her competent, professional brand of nursing. According to Dunn, who had set up a field hospital in a nearby home during the battle, "We had expended every bandage, torn up every sheet in the house, and everything we could find, when who should drive up but our old friend Miss Barton, with a team loaded down with dressings of every kind, and everything we could ask for. She distributed her articles to the difference hospitals, worked all night making soup, all the next day and night, and when I left, four days after the battle, I left her there ministering to the wounded and the dying. When I returned to the field-hospital last week, she was still at work, supplying them with delicacies of every kind, and administering to their wants, all of which she does out of her own private fortune."

Dunn concluded his letter with these fateful words: "Now, what do you think of Miss Barton? In my feeble estimation, Gen. McClellan, with all his laurels, sinks into insignificance beside the true heroine of the age, the angel of the battlefield." When the letter made its way into the newspapers in the North, Barton's new nickname stuck and defined her reputation for the rest of her life.

Pete Unseth's picture of the monument to Barton at Antietam, featuring a piece of her home in the form of a red cross

In early 1863, Barton's brother David was sent by the Army to Hilton Head, South Carolina, to serve as quartermaster, and hoping to get deeper into the South and thus closer to the action, Clara sought and received permission to go with him. On March 29, Edward V. Preston, a recently appointed paymaster, wrote the following to Dr Von Etten, the Medical Director for Union Forces on St Helena Island, at Port Royal, South Carolina: "The bearer Miss Clara H. Barton visits the 10th Army Corps for the purpose of attending personally to the wants of wounded soldiers. She has rendered great service in all the great battles that have been fought in Virginia for the last six months. She acts under the direction of the Surgeon General and with the authority of the Secretary of War. The smoke of battle, the roar of artillery, and the shrieks of shot and shell do not deter her from administering to those who fall. She will explain all to you and I trust he able to do much good in the coming battle. Here she is highly respected and all bestow upon her much praise. If in your power to assist her in carrying out her plans, please do all that can be done and rest assured your kindness will be appreciated."

Shortly after they arrived in South Carolina, Barton met Colonel John Johnson Elwell, who had heard she was coming and made arrangements for her housing. According to a 2018 article published by the National Museum of Civil War Medicine, "Elwell, the Chief Quartermaster for the Department of the South…graduated from Cleveland Medical College in 1846 and practiced medicine in Orwell, OH, for several years. In 1846, he married Nancy Chittenden and they had four children, none of whom survived childhood…At the outbreak of war, Elwell was appointed to the Quartermaster department…"

Elwell's marital status aside, he and Barton appear to have become romantically involved. At 42, Barton was certainly old enough to know that she had no future with a married man, but she still allowed the relationship to develop to such a strong and public level that they posed together in a photograph taken by the renowned photographer Matthew Brady. Unfortunately, any news, or even just gossip, about their relationship would undermine not only Barton's own mission, but the future of women serving alongside men in combat, or even just near combat situations. While nothing permanent ever came of their relationship, they continued to correspond for the rest of Elwell's life.

Elwell

Meanwhile, Barton continued to work for the soldiers, and in 1864, Union General Benjamin Butler appointed her "lady in charge" of field hospitals for the Army of the James. On June 2 of that year, M. M. Marsh, Superintendent for the U.S. Sanitary Commission, wrote to her, "Expect to see you Monday next. I wish to consult you upon the propriety of establishing a place at the 'Head' where discharged soldiers and others could rendezvous for lodging and subsistence. Also to ask, if such a thing should be established, if you would not assume its general supervision, Etc."

Barton's work on the battlefield was not without danger, for she was often tending soldiers during the fighting itself. This required her to moved quickly from soldier to soldier, always in a crouched position, with her long dress and petticoats dragging along the grass. If heavy rain came, the water would wick up into her skirts, making the already heavy garments even more cumbersome. Furthermore, while she might have a young orderly with to carry her bandages, she often had to carry as many supplies as she could on her person, dragging her haversack from patient to patient. She soon became an expert at what would now be called triage, determining if a soldier was dead or past help, or if he should be taken to the field station. Every patient put orderlies in danger, so she could not waste their efforts on a dead man.

The seriousness of her situation was always on her mind, but never as much as when a bullet passed through the sleeve of her own dress, grown loose through hard work and short rations, and struck the man she was tending, killing him instantly without leaving a mark on her. She recalled, "A ball had passed between my body and the right arm which supported him, cutting through the sleeve and passing through his chest from shoulder to shoulder. There was no more to be done for him and I left him to his rest. I have never mended that hole in my sleeve."

For all that she built her reputation with her work on the battlefield, Barton arguably rendered an even greater service right as the war was ending. In 1865, letters began to pour in to her home address begging her for any information she might have about soldiers who had failed to write back or who were otherwise missing and presumed dead. In many cases, these men had been buried in unmarked graves on battlefields, and while some who were listed as missing were actually dead, no one had confirmed their demise.

In response, Barton appealed to the government to allow her to try to find out what happened to these men. In one of his last acts before his assassination in April 1865, President Abraham Lincoln suggested that she move to Annapolis, Maryland, through which most prisoners of war would pass on their way home. Once there, she could begin to make of list of those who came through, as well as notes concerning those believed to be dead. In his own words, Lincoln sent out a simple advertisement: "To the friends of missing persons; Miss Clara Barton has kindly offered to search for the missing prisoners of war. Please address her at Annapolis, Maryland, giving name, regiment, and company of any missing prisoner."

The *Washington Chronicle* also carried this announcement: "Notice to the Friends of Paroled and Exchanged Prisoners.—In view of the great anxiety felt throughout the country for the welfare of our prisoners now arriving at Annapolis, Maryland, Miss Clara Barton, by permission of General Hitchcock, Commissioner of Exchange, with the sanction of the President, has kindly undertaken to furnish information, by correspondence, in regard to the condition of our returned soldiers, and especially those in the hospitals at Annapolis; and, so far as it may be possible, to learn the facts connected with those who have died in prison and elsewhere. All letters addressed to Miss Clara Barton, Annapolis, Maryland, will meet with prompt attention. Editors throughout the country are requested to copy this notice.— Wash. Chronicle"

Thanks to these efforts, Barton compiled a list of more than 20,000 soldiers who died in battle, and the list was sent to post offices nationwide. Based on her success, she moved back to Washington and created the "Bureau of Correspondence for Friends of Paroled Prisoners," using $7,000 of her own money to hire 12 clerks to help her answer every piece of correspondence. There she perfected a system of recordkeeping that would be used in future wars.

On June 21, 1865, the *Alexandria Soldiers Journal* praised her work: "Miss Clara Barton has hit upon an excellent device for bringing to the knowledge of friends the fate or whereabouts of missing soldiers. Some weeks ago she published an invitation to the public to send to her address, in this city, a description of missing soldiers, giving the name, regiment, company, and the State to which they respectively belong. In response, she has already received such descriptions of some thousands. Roll No. 1 is a large sheet, containing, we believe, about fifteen hundred names of missing prisoners of war. Twenty thousand copies of this roll have been printed and circulated all through the loyal States, and among the camps; and she now calls upon soldiers and others who can give information concerning the missing men to write to her immediately. Great care should be taken to write the name and address in every instance plainly. Her plan is highly appreciated and approved by the War Department and by the President. All letters must be directed to Miss Clara Barton, Washington, D. C."

When her own money ran out, Barton appealed to Congress for $15,000 to keep the work going. On March 2, 1866, the Senate Committee on Military Affairs and the Militia issued the following report: "That on the arrival at Annapolis of large numbers of paroled and exchanged prisoners of war, in the winter of 1864-5, she received letters of inquiry from all parts of the country, desiring information of soldiers supposed to have been captured. She then advertised, with the entire approval of President Lincoln, that she would receive and answer such letters from Annapolis; and by publication of the names of missing soldiers and personal inquiry among the prisoners, she received information of more than one thousand of the fifteen hundred soldiers whose names were thus published, and which she communicated without delay to their anxious relatives. She subsequently found it necessary on account of the largely increased number of inquiries, to extend her labors and incur additional expense, by the employment of clerks, and the publication of additional lists of missing men, 20,000 of which were distributed through the country, including one copy to each post office in the loyal states."

The report continued, "The system which she has originated has thus far proved a complete success, but she has been compelled to abandon the project solely for lack of means to carry it on; and in order to enable her to carry it to completion, the committee respectfully recommend the passage of the accompanying joint resolution appropriating $15,000 to reimburse her for expense already incurred, and to aid her in completing her work…The only aid she has heretofore received has been the printing of the rolls by the public printer, which the joint resolution recommends shall be continued."

Ultimately, the report concluded, "She has in many instances obtained information of soldiers who were reported as "deserters," while they were languishing in southern prisons, and their families were mourning for them as disgraced, and her report has carried joy to many a household, whose members, while they may have had presumptive evidence of the capture or death of the absent one, only received positive evidence through her instrumentality. Her observation warrants her in stating that, if the desired aid be granted, information can be obtained of probably four-fifths of those whose fate will otherwise never be ascertained. The committee therefore respectfully recommend the passage of the accompanying resolution."

As part of her work in the Office of Missing Soldiers, Barton came in contact with Dorence Atwater, who had been a prisoner of war at Andersonville for 11 months. It seems that Atwater had kept his own list of Union dead and, upon reading Barton's published list, realized that there were quite a few men who were listed as missing that he knew had died in the Civil War's most notorious prison camp. Atwater got in touch with Barton, and together they formulated a plan to travel to Andersonville to identify and mark the graves of those buried there.

That is how they ended up in the sweltering Georgia heat. It was not easy to travel through the South, where so much of the local infrastructure had been destroyed by Union forces, and one Georgia newspaper reported in mid-June, "In yesterday s paper we noticed the arrival of the United States Steamer Virginia from Washington laden with headboards and fencing for the graves of the Union prisoners who died in the Andersonville stockade. From the misapprehension existing in Washington as to the state of the railroads in Georgia the present time the movement was made somewhat prematurely and it is doubtful if the expedition attempts to go further at this time…The mission started from Washington, however, under the most favorable auspices. The most reliable information for the guidance of the work was in possession of the projects while the War Department cheerfully accorded every assistance. One of the most efficient and earnest of the volunteer laborers in the Hospitals and on the battlefields of the War one of those noble women whose heroic devotion has added á new glory to American womanhood. Miss Clara Barton, a name which hereafter is to hold a place beside those of Florence Nightingale and Miss Dix, accompanied the party."

The work took most of the summer. On August 2, Barton wrote to her uncle that "we are fairly at work, and up to the present time have consigned to their last resting place 6,822 of our noble defenders.— Denham avenue, through the centre of the grounds…is forty feet wide, and lined on both sides with plants brought by Captain Moore from Arlington Cemetery…The grounds are nearly all enclosed, and I fear I shall have to dispatch Capt. James M. Moore to Washington for an additional supply of headboards, as those we brought with us are nearly exhausted..."

A Celebrity at Home and Abroad

An engraving of Barton

"Everybody's business is nobody's business, and nobody's business is my business." – Clara Barton

Following the war, Barton spent several years traveling around the country giving well-received talks on her experiences during the Civil War. This was a huge step for the tiny woman who had once been afraid to meet new neighbors, and during this time, Barton met a number of influential people who encouraged her in her work and whom she in turn encouraged. Among them was Susan B. Anthony, with whom she shared the common interest of expanding women's rights in the United States. Barton went on to support Anthony's work and that of others, often speaking in favor of women's suffrage.

Anthony

On one occasion, she spoke an audience of some 400 who had come to hear her speak after an advertisement preceding the event warned, "We can promise our citizens a rare treat of patriotic eloquence, such as is seldom listened to, and we can assure them that there will be no cause for disappointment; they will not have thrust upon them a lecture about women's rights after the style of Susan B. Anthony and her clique. Miss Barton does not belong to that class of woman." Instead, she assured them, "That paragraph, my comrades, does worse than misrepresent me as a woman; it maligns my friend. It abuses the highest and bravest work ever done in this land for either you or me. You glorify the women who made their way to the front to reach you in your misery, and nursed you back to life. You called us angels. Who opened the way for women to go, and made it possible? Who but that detested clique who through years of opposition, toil and pain had openly claimed that women had rights and should have the privilege to exercise them — the right to her own property, her own children, her own home, her just individual claim before the law, to her freedom of action, to her personal liberty."

During this period, Barton also became acquainted with Frederick Douglass, with whom she also formed a lasting friendship. In April 1869, he thanked her for her continued support of civil rights for those recently freed from the shackles of slavery: "In fulfillment of your promise to write me the result of your interview with General Butler: I sincerely thank you for this letter. It tells me anew, of your devotion to suffering humanity is every form and of every Colour. While in the west, I saw a paper in which it was stated that you have already opened an establishment in Washington to gain employment to destitute colored women willing and able to work. I have seen nothing on the subject since. Your energy, zeal and influence lead me to believe that you are successfully at work...I hope to be in Washington soon and will there be very glad to see you and learn all about the good work in which you are engaged...Believe you how [sic] Gen'l Butler as powerful in action as in word. It was a huge undertaking for you to encounter this General and seek to [sic] his judgement on the side of your wisely benevolent enterprise and much have been exceedingly gratifying to you, as it certainly is to me, to know."

Douglass

While Barton was able to accomplish much during this period in her life, she was still limited by an obstacle that many such individuals have had to contend with: government bureaucracy. In "Finding Clara Barton," an article published in *The Humanist* in 2018, Luis Granados wrote of her efforts, "The trouble was, the army was doing the same thing, at the same time--the army way. There was an ugly dispute about who was entitled to a list of Andersonville prisoners one of Barton's friends had found, that…made her look bad. There were also her increasingly vocal demands in the press for federal funding…in an amount many thought was unjustifiably large. The…work of her office ended abruptly when she suffered a nervous breakdown."

Knowing that her celebrity would make it nearly impossible for her to get any real rest in America, Barton's doctors recommended she travel to Europe. The money she had earned from her talks allowed her to travel in comfort, and in 1869 she arrived in Geneva, Switzerland, where mutual friends introduced her to Dr. Louis Appia. Appia was a Swiss military surgeon who, along with four others, had established the "Committee of Five" in 1863. The group was committed to improving the quality of care given to large groups of people during times of war or crisis, and it later became known as the International Committee of the Red Cross.

Appia

Appia saw in Barton a kindred soul and encouraged her to take news of their endeavors home with her to America. During this period, she also read *A Memory of Solferino* by Henry Dunant, which called on world leaders to form a politically neutral society to serve all people in crisis equally.

When France and Germany went to war in 1870, Barton, sensing another opportunity to help people, went to Germany to offer her assistance, and there she met a woman who would change her life. In her early biography, *Clara Barton, Humanitarian*, Corra Bacon Foster explained, "Princess Louise, Grand Duchess of Baden, only daughter of King William of Prussia, came into the life of Clara Barton at this time in a personal visit to her...This royal lady came to urge her to go to Karlsruhe to counsel and assist in directing Red Cross work for relief." Together, the two women set up military hospitals and assisted the Red Cross in its efforts to bring resources to the area.

Princess Louise

In an unusual turn of events, authorities from both France and Germany asked the Red Cross for help. Foster continued, "[Barton] served on several battle-fields, including Worth and Gravelotte, and entered Strassburg immediately after the surrender to find a scene of devastation and misery rarely equalled...with the earnest cooperation of the Grand Duchess of Baden, she procured materials for clothing, cutters, and teachers, secured a large room for work and invited women to come and make clothing for themselves and others and also earn a moderate pay therefor. For eight months fifteen hundred finished garments were turned out weekly. She also organized relief work at Metz, Montbelard, and Belfort."

Not only did Barton serve the soldiers, but she set the tone for the future work of the Red Cross by serving individuals suffering from the war's aftereffects, arriving in Strasburg just after the Siege of Paris. Foster explained, "After the fall of the Paris Commune, May, 1871, Clara Barton went to that distressed city with the International Red Cross relief workers with supplies, including garments that had been made in Strasburg. She also distributed in France funds from the French Relief committees of Boston." Barton's efforts earned her both the Iron Cross from Prussia and the Golden Cross of Baden.

According to Foster, as cold weather set in, Barton "went to Karlsruhe, becoming there a member of the 'palace set,' an intimate companion of the Grand Duchess of Baden. The following summer she made an extended tour with friends in Italy. Her health again failing, she spent a year of illness in London, returning to America late in 1873." She continued to suffer from various illnesses until finally, in 1876, she took up residence in a sanitorium in Dansville, New York for 10 years.

That said, just because she was ill did not mean she was idle. According to Granados, "Barton returned home obsessed with getting the United States to join that treaty. This was far harder than it sounds. Every American knew George Washington's dictum to "avoid foreign entanglements." Besides, we weren't going to be in any more wars like the Civil War, so what was the point? Barton shrewdly expanded the Red Cross mission to include victims of natural disasters, and kept hammering away at her lobbying campaign with well-publicized efforts to provide immediate relief after floods and hurricanes. Some of Barton's other firsts are difficult to prove, but she was unquestionably the first woman to lead a successful decade-long lobbying campaign of this magnitude."

As a result, Barton devoted her years of rest to writing copious letters encouraging the United States government to recognize the International Committee of the Red Cross (ICRC). In 1878, she even left the sanitarium long enough to meet with President Rutherford B. Hayes. Asserting that the Red Cross was of best use during a time of military conflict, such as the Civil War, and that America would never face such a disaster again, Hayes dismissed her suggestions. However, as was her custom, Barton refused to give up and continued to fight, ultimately impressing Hayes' successor, Chester Arthur, with her argument that the Red Cross would indeed serve the country during peacetime in response to natural disasters such as hurricanes and earthquakes.

Arthur

The American Red Cross

"An institution or reform movement that is not selfish, must originate in the recognition of some evil that is adding to the sum of human suffering, or diminishing the sum of happiness." – Clara Barton

By the time American Red Cross held its first meeting on May 21, 1881, Barton was well enough to travel to Washington, D.C. and become its president. Just a few months later, the first local society met near Barton's country home in Danville, New York, on August 22.

Despite being ready to hit the ground running, the organization might have fallen into disuse had a flooding Ohio River not wreaked havoc a few years later. In 2017, an article in *American History Magazine* told readers, "In February 1884, torrential rain and unseasonably warm temperatures brought the icy waters of the Ohio River to a deadly roil. The resulting flood inundated villages, towns and cities along the nearly 1,000-mile-long Ohio Valley, leaving tens of thousands of people without food, heat or shelter. Downstream, the Ohio's surging waters flowed into the Mississippi River and caused it to crash through its levees. Clara

Barton…jumped into action...Now she saw an opportunity to expand the American Red Cross mission into largely uncharted territory: providing aid during a natural catastrophe."

According to the article, the Red Cross executed an "unprecedented, four-month relief effort during the Great Flood of 1884 and the hazards she and volunteers faced traveling 8,000 miles on the rivers, between Cincinnati and New Orleans, to distribute $175,000 in charitable supplies to those affected by the disaster" were memorable.

Writing in "The Red Cross in Peace and War," Barton described the work: "It had not been my intention to remain at the scene of disaster, but rather to see, investigate, establish an agency and return to national headquarters at Washington. But I might also say, in military parlance, that I was "surprised and captured." The government had placed its military boats upon the river to rescue the people and issue rations. But they provided neither fuel nor clothing...The people were more likely to freeze than starve and against this there was no provision. We quickly removed our headquarters from Cincinnati to Evansville, 300 miles below and at the head of the recent scene of disaster. A new staunch steamer of four hundred tons was immediately chartered and laden with clothing and coal; the Red Cross flag was hoisted and, amid surging waters and crashing ice, the clear-toned bell and shrill whistle of the "Josh V. Throop" announced to the generous inhabitants of a noble city that from the wharves of Evansville the Red Cross was putting out the first relief boat that ever floated on American waters."

The Red Cross followed up on its work in Ohio by lending aid to people starving in Texas. Barton later wrote in her *Story of the American Red Cross,* "Before the close of the following year, 1885, came what was known as the 'Texas Famine'… In mid-winter, 1886…we proceeded to Albany, Texas, made headquarters—traveled over the stricken counties, found wretchedness, hunger, thirst, cold, heart-breaking discouragement. The third year of drought was upon them...The condition was pitiful. To them it was hopeless." Then, thanks to Barton's intervention, "A column of editorial told the true situation. A modest contribution of the Red Cross headed a subscription list, General Belo following with his, and almost immediately the legislature made an appropriation of one hundred thousand dollars for food and supplies. The tender-hearted and conscience-smitten people sent their donations. Our task was done. We had seen and conquered."

The Red Cross had yet another opportunity to show its usefulness in the wake of February 19, 1888, when a tornado swept through Mount Vernon, Illinois, killing more than 100 people and leaving more than a thousand homeless. Writing for the Southern Illinoisan, Becky Malkovich discussed the disaster: "The city's plight gained national attention with the arrival of American Red Cross founder Clara Barton. A hospital was set up in the appellate courthouse, mostly spared as the tornado whipped across the city. While Barton brought with her $150,000 worth of supplies, she put out a plea for funds to help the city in its recovery. 'The pitiless snow is falling on the heads of people who are without homes, without food and without clothing,' she wrote.

More than $100,000 was donated for the efforts and donations of materials and supplies were also sent to the city. A supply center was set up at the city's Presbyterian church, its location near the railroad, making it a convenient repository for the donations that would soon pour in from around the country, like the boxcar filled with flour donated by the citizens of Fargo, N.D."

Later in 1888, when a Yellow Fever epidemic swept through North Florida in September, Barton once again sprang into action by sending about 20 New Orleans nurses to the scene. She later wrote, "Our place was in Washington, to receive, deal carefully with, and hold back the tide of offered service from the hundreds of enthusiastic, excited untrained volunteers, rushing on to danger and death…The supplies forwarded by us were estimated at ten thousand dollars. The money received was $6,281.58. Out of this sum we paid our twenty nurses three dollars a day, for seventy-nine days—their cost of living, and their transportation when needed. We paid our doctor in charge twenty dollars a day, the customary price, for the same period." She then offered this account of the rest of her expenses: "We paid our office rent, assistants, telegraphing, drayage for supplies sent on by us (railroad transportation free), and all incidentals for a relief work of over three months' duration. This ran our debit column over on the other side over one thousand dollars. Our little part of the relief of that misfortune was estimated at fifteen thousand dollars, and only those relieved were more grateful than we."

Although floods rarely get as much coverage as other kinds of natural disasters like volcanic explosions, the Johnstown Flood of 1889 has remained an exception due to the sheer destruction and magnitude of the disaster. On May 31, 1889, Johnstown became a casualty of a combination of heavy rains and the failure of the South Fork Dam to stem the rising water levels of Lake Conemaugh about 15 miles away. The dam's inability to contain the water and its subsequent collapse resulted in a catastrophic flood that swept through the town with virtually no warning. With water flowing at a rate equivalent to the Mississippi River, a tide of water and debris 60 feet high and traveling 40 miles per hour in some places surged through Johnstown and swept away people and property alike. The flood ultimately resulted in the deaths of over 2,000 people and destroyed thousands of buildings, wreaking damages estimated to be the equivalent of nearly half a billion dollars today.

In 1889, the Johnstown Flood was the deadliest natural disaster in American history, and though it was later surpassed by other events, the unprecedented nature of the flood led to relief efforts never before seen, including by the Red Cross. The Johnstown Flood also led to a change in laws as people tried and failed to recoup damages caused by the collapse of the dam and the subsequent flood.

In response to the disastrous flood, Barton was able to get 50 doctors and nurses on the scene within a few days of the waters receding. Writing for Johnstown's *Tribune Democrat* in 2014, Kelly Urban observed, "The Johnstown Flood claimed more than 2,000 lives and left substantial wreckage in its wake. But it didn't take long for Barton and the 50 doctors, nurses and relief workers to quickly set up feeding stations, and they immediately began providing medical care, shelter and relief...Barton quickly arranged for construction of Red Cross hotels to provide lodging for homeless flood survivors. The first was built on the site of the destroyed St. Mark's Episcopal Church on Locust Street...Because of its success, the American Red Cross built five more hotels and 3,000 single family homes...4,700 of the town's destitute took shelter in these homes the winter after the flood."

Unfortunately, by this time competition and professional jealousy between Red Cross organizations had reared its ugly head. Urban continued, "A day after Barton and her crew arrived in Johnstown, Dr. William H. Pancoast, president of the Associate Society of the Red Cross of Philadelphia, arrived...despite a disagreement between Barton and Pancoast, both chapters coordinated relief efforts – Pancoast's group tending to the medical needs of flood victims and Barton's people providing food, shelter and furniture...The Red Cross distributed supplies and housing materials valued at nearly $200,000 and spent $39,000...Barton and the other American Red Cross workers stayed in Johnstown until the fall. She left on Oct. 24, 1889, and the people of Johnstown gave her a gold pen and a locket, set in diamonds and amethysts, as a farewell present." Regarding her time in Johnstown, Barton later described its inhabitants as "a people as patient and brave as people are made, as noble and grateful as falls to the lot of human nature to be. Enterprising, industrious and hopeful, the new Johnstown, phoenix-like, rose from its ruins more beautiful than the old...God bless her and God bless all who helped save her!"

Picture of damage in the lower part of Johnstown a few days after the flood

Remarks such as these have led many people to assume that Barton was a devout Christian. In fact, the Young Reader's Christian Library published a biography of her in 1999 in which her Christian virtues were extolled. For her own part, Barton considered herself a Universalist but never joined any church. In 1905, near the end of her life, she wrote to a friend, "Your belief that I am a Universalist is as correct as your greater belief that you are one yourself, a belief in which all who are privileged to possess it rejoice. In my case, it was a great gift, like St. Paul, I 'was born free', and saved the pain of reaching it through years of struggle and doubt...Your historic records will show that the old Huguenot town of Oxford, Mass. erected one of, if not the first Universalist Church in America. In this town I was born; in this church I was reared. In all its reconstructions and remodelings I have taken a part, and I look anxiously for a time in the near future when the busy world will let me once more become a living part of its people, praising God for the advance in the liberal faith of the religions of the world today, so largely due to the teachings of this belief."

On the other hand, Granados speculated that she may have been more of what is today called a humanist: "We know that she never worked through the auspices of any church, though life might have been easier if she had...We also know that she liked to call herself a 'well-disposed pagan.' Some of her letters and talks expressed a standard nineteenth-century hope that God would do this or that, but there is no doubting the firmness of her conviction that wounded soldiers didn't need prayers--they needed water. That sounds pretty humanist."

In 1897, Barton recognized a rare opportunity to demonstrate to the world the truly international nature of the Red Cross. Historian Michael Hoffman explained, "On December 2, 1895 [,] Clara Barton was approaching her 74th birthday and, presumably, the end of her career; and on this date President Cleveland presented his annual message to Congress. His report on foreign relations included this update: 'Occurrences in Turkey have continued to excite concern'...President Cleveland noted that no harm had come to U.S. citizens thus far, though significant damage had been done to their property. He also pointedly took note that European powers had the responsibility to 'interfere,' if necessary, on behalf of endangered Christians...Perhaps uniquely for a woman in that day, Clara Barton was seen as the natural leader for an American relief effort. She was approached to lead an expedition into the Armenian provinces of the Ottoman Empire...She was persuaded, and left from New York in January 1896 on a journey that took her...ultimately to Constantinople to begin her humanitarian work. She was accompanied by four colleagues also representing the American Red Cross, Dr. Julian Hubbell, George Pullman, Lucy Graves, and Ernest Mason."

Their mission was difficult but straightforward: "to convert cash donations into urgently needed relief for the Armenian people. Her challenge was to maintain humanitarian neutrality, neither siding with the cheering crowd who saw her off in New York and other American supporters of the Armenian people, nor demonstrating animus to the Ottoman authorities, whose approval and support was indispensable for her mission to succeed."

From the beginning, their work was met with opposition. As Barton delicately put it, "A week at sea, to be met at midnight in Southampton, by messenger down from London, to say that the prohibition was sustained, the Red Cross was forbidden, but that such persons as our Minister, Mr. Terrell, would appoint, would be received. Here was another delicate uncertainty which could not be committed to Ottoman telegraph; and Dr. Hubbell was dispatched alone to Constantinople..." Fortunately, "Under favorable responses we proceeded, and reached Constantinople on February 15th; met with a cordial reception from all our own government officials, and located pro tem at Pera Palace Hotel; it being so recently after the Stamboul massacres that no less public place was deemed safe."

When Barton met with the Turkish Minister of Foreign Affairs, she described the kind of work she would be doing, and how it would help the Ottoman government. She also assured him that her people "would embrace plows, hoes, spades, seed-corn, wheat, and later, sickles, scythes, etc. for harvesting, with which to save the miles of autumn grain which we had heard of as growing on the great plains already in the ground before the trouble; also to provide for them such cattle and other animals as it would be possible to purchase or to get back; that if some such thing were not done before another winter, unless we had been greatly misinformed, the suffering there would shock the entire civilized world." Finally, she added that "humanity alone would be their guide," and that there would be no publicity surrounding her efforts. She closed by promising that the Red Cross intended to act with "truth, fairness, and integrity."

Hoffman mentioned the impact she had with this effort: "Barton's approach, coming at the dawn of modern humanitarian practice, and anticipating practice to follow into our own time, won the approval...She directed operations from Constantinople, utilizing the Ottoman telegraph system to communicate with her teams in the field. Beginning in March and through that summer, four red cross expeditions set out to relieve Armenian communities ravaged by recent massacres, and not free from like dangers ahead...they provided medical support to quell epidemics, provided food, and helped rebuild food security by purchasing and delivering the agricultural implements and livestock that Barton had promised...The expeditions encountered destruction everywhere and, sometimes, threats of fresh violence to themselves, as well as the Armenian people."

Barton had hardly completed her work overseas when the United States once again needed her help after the Spanish American War broke out on April 21, 1898. Providentially, Barton was on the scene before the war even began in earnest. Writing in 2011 for the *Florida Atlantic Comparative Studies Journal*, historian Christine Ardadlan explained, "In the midst of bringing Red Cross aid to those suffering through disasters at home and abroad, news of the Cuban *reconcentrados* plight distressed Barton...She argued that the Red Cross was a 'direct servant of the government,' therefore, without President William McKinley's permission, Barton would not endorse any Red Cross involvement. Cuban patriots…attacked Barton and the Red Cross for inhumanity towards the *reconcentrados*."

Finally, in 1897, Barton asked that "the Red Cross take steps on its own in direct touch and with the cooperation of the people of the country" to help the refugees. She also met with President McKinley and persuaded him to create a "President's Committee for Cuban Relief."

McKinley's one request was that Barton herself oversee the work. That is how she ended up in Cuba nearly a year before the war began.

Ardadlan continued, "Upon arrival three days later, the hunger and starvation that had permeated the small villages overrun with people suffering from years of want struck Barton to the quick...She set to work visiting sites where the Red Cross could arrange distribution centers. The Red Cross hospital's chief nurse Bettina Hofker Lesser, Dr. Monae A. Lesser and four nurses from the now closed Red Cross Hospital followed Barton to Cuba to support her work…On February 15, 1898, Clara Barton…worked at her desk overlooking Havana Harbor. The 77-year old president and founder of the American Red Cross (ARC) pondered over her relief effort to bring aid to displaced Cubans—the reconcentrados. From her window, she witnessed the commotion. The United States Battleship Maine had exploded and sunk in Havana Harbor with 250 men dead. After the blast, she made her way to the bruised, cut and burned survivors at the Spanish Military Hospital, San Ambrosia."

Alerting the Red Cross, Barton cabled them, "I am with the wounded." Drawing on her experience following the Civil War, she immediately began recording the names of every soldier she encountered, even as she rendered first aid. She reported back, "Their wounds are all over them—heads and faces terribly cut, internal wounds, arms, legs, feet and hands burned to the live flesh. The hair and beards singed, showing that the burns were from fire not steam. Besides further evidence shows that the burns are where the parts were uncovered. If burned by steam the clothing would have held the steam and burned all the deeper."

For all that the Red Cross was a neutral organization, Barton could still appreciate the power of political machinations and the way in which they could affect her humanitarian efforts. Ardadlan noted, "Highlighting its humanity and neutrality, she reported about her cooperation with the Spanish authorities. Spain was one of the original founders of the International Red Cross and Barton fostered a rapport with General Ramón Blanco y Erenas." Barton reported that the general "was glad of this relief and sorry for the condition of the people." This was an important move because it emphasized that the Red Cross was indeed politically neutral and would not take a side in this conflict, despite being an American organization.

Ardadlan described what happened next: "Two days before the outbreak of war, the Red Cross relief ship, the State of Texas, left New York harbor full of supplies for the reconcentrados. Barton was anxious that the Geneva Convention did not cover naval warfare at this time...On April 29th, Barton joined the State of Texas in Key West. She begged Admiral Sampson to allow it to pass the blockade surrounding the island. Admiral Sampson declared it his duty to keep the supplies out of the country. Barton insisted it was her duty to get them in! She had no choice but to wait patiently in Tampa where the troops gathered to depart for Cuba. Although tedious, the wait was not without action. Barton and her staff turned their attention to the Spanish crew of vessels, offering them sustenance under the auspices of the Red Cross. Again, 'ease suffering' was her philosophy. She explained that until then 'they had only live fish and brown sugar to eat.'"

The Red Cross was not the only organization mobilizing in Tampa. Groups from all over the country, made up largely of men and women who had grown up with tales of the glories of the Civil War, some of which Barton herself had told, were rushing there to fight or help with the fighting, according to their gender, age and talents. Unlike during the Civil War, America now boasted scores of well-trained female nurses, and many flocked to Tampa to be part of the action. Once they got there, the Red Cross not only welcomed them but also offered to pay them for their services. Adadlon concluded, "Finally, when war arrived, functioning under the realm of humanitarian relief, Barton followed Theodore Roosevelt and the Rough Riders to Guantanamo Bay."

It did not take long, however, for people to believe that a 77-year-old woman, or any woman regardless of her background for that matter, could be of much value in a battlefield hospital. Discouraged, Barton confided to her diary on June 24, 1898, "Some of their surgeons called on us; all seemed interested in the Red Cross, but none thought that a woman nurse would be in place in a soldier's hospital; indeed, very much out of place. I suggested that that decision was hard for me, for I had spent a great deal of time there myself. They appeared to understand that perfectly, or were so polite as not to criticise it, but there seemed to be a later line which could not be crossed. The Cubans, who had just come into camp, were less conventional and expressed a great desire for any assistance we could give them. 'Sister Bettina' and her four trained 'Sisters,' Drs. Egan and Hubbell went ashore to the hospitals."

In the end, efficiency won the day, and Barton concluded her entry by writing that "as soon as [the nurses] were fairly in the wards they commenced putting things into order and cleanliness, and worked through the day without interruption...Long before that day's work was ended our own American hospitals alongside commenced to be jealous of the Cubans, and believed that they had spoken first. Be that as it might, we were equally forgetful, and from that time no distinction between the hospitals was known."

Barton served in Tampa for more than a month before she finally received permission to head to a battlefield. According to Adadlon, "On the second day of the July 3rd San Juan battle, Barton received a message that the wounded desperately needed care at the battlefront. Ensuring the supplies were loaded in the only two wagons available, she commandeered a hay wagon and proceeded over hills to a valley surrounded by dense jungle and mountains. She reached a collection of tents, the First Division Hospital of the Fifth Army Corps."

It did not take Barton long to evaluate the situation and determine that the surroundings were antithetical to survival. Indeed, accustomed as she was to war on a large continent, nothing could prepare her for what it looked like in a jungle environment. She vividly described what she encountered: "Wounded men lay everywhere, exposed to the tropical elements made worse than ever by the rainy season. More than eight hundred men were 'recovering' from surgery, some sheltered by palm leaves, many lying naked, in pools of water, exposed to the elements." Some men, who knew her by reputation, cried out, 'There is a woman! …My God, boys, It's Clara Barton. Now we'll get something to eat.'"

As that account indicated, there were few women near the front. In fact, Barton was the only female nurse approved to be there, and she wasted no time setting up an emergency room and trying to provide care. Vowing to nurse soldiers from either side, Barton came in for criticism among some Americans, but she continued on with her cause, and whatever bitterness she felt remained with her and her journal.

Barton recorded in her diary one exchange with an American Major.

> Major: You have been to the front. I should think you find it very unpleasant there. There is no need of your going there—it is no place for women. I consider women very much out of place in a field hospital.
>
> Barton, after recounting to him some of her experiences: I must have been out of place a good deal, Doctor, for I have been [in the battlefield] a great deal.
>
> Major: That doesn't change my opinion, if I had my way I would send you home,

Barton's full furor did not find permanent record, which was perhaps a good thing. Still, as Adadlon noted, "Throughout the war, Barton's team was continually overwhelmed with the amount of work. The army's meager resources did little to supplement Red Cross supplies. In fact, Red Cross supplies targeting for starving Cubans went to supply the army. Nurse reinforcements recruited by the New York committee arrived in eastern Cuba, but the army refused them permission to land. To Barton, most trying of all was her continual struggle to maintain her authority to administer care at the battlefront…Outbreaks of disease, malaria, yellow fever, typhoid and dysentery posed such a problem [Surgeon General George M.] Sternberg allowed female nurses to attend the camps and the hospital transport ships. The New York Red Cross sent 700 nurses to the camps and hospitals."

Barton's final mission on behalf of the Red Cross took place in 1900, the dawn of a new century that her work would help shape. She was 79 when she traveled to Galveston, Texas, following the deadliest hurricane in American history. Prior to advanced communications, few people knew about impending hurricanes except those closest to the site, and in the days before television, or even radio, catastrophic descriptions were merely recorded on paper, limiting an understanding of the immediate impact. Stories could be published after the water receded and the dead were buried, but by then, the immediate shock had worn off and all that remained were the memories of the survivors. Thus, it was inevitable that the Category 4 hurricane wrought almost inconceivable destruction as it made landfall in Texas with winds at 145 miles per hour.

Due to the lack of technology and warning, many of the people it killed were never identified, and the nameless corpses were eventually burned in piles of bodies that could not be interred due to the soggy soil. Others were simply buried at sea. The second deadliest hurricane in American history claimed 2,500 lives, so it's altogether possible that the Galveston hurricane killed over four times more than the next deadliest in the nation. To this day, it remains America's deadliest natural disaster.

In "Clara Barton and the Formation of Public Policy in Galveston, 1900," Elizabeth Hayes discussed the help Barton and the Red Cross provided: "The Galveston disaster of September 8, 1900, coming just three months after Red Cross incorporation, presented an opportunity for Barton to once again demonstrate her mettle in the field and to elevate the Red Cross to the position of undisputed leading charitable organization for emergency relief in the United States...When news of the crisis in Galveston reached her, she responded immediately and valiantly by rushing to the island, by bringing in over $100,000 in money and goods for the relief effort, and by distributing items to thousands of homeless, destitute, and grieving residents of the island. The results of her presence in Galveston, however, went far beyond the immediate relief needs of the people. In her dealings with city officials, she carefully crafted a socially progressive role for middle-class white women, attempted to set a more positive example for race relations, and, after her vast experience with disaster survivors, introduced concepts of permanent individual housing for the homeless...While her relationship with the all-male Central Relief Committee was cordial, there were moments in her six-week stay when she pushed her own vision of a restored Galveston onto the committee and chided them for their insensitivity. While others may have seen Clara Barton as too old or too old fashioned, she should be considered progressive in her ability to see beyond southern cultural limitations and to act in accordance with her broad experience."

Still, Hayes pointed out that this was "her last field experience...Whereas her critics viewed her as difficult to work with -- employing personal methods of administering relief goods and irregular accounting methods -- southern historians might well see another side to her personality and to her contributions to Galveston's recovery. As a woman raised in the North with a broad national reputation, she brought to Galveston a more enlightened vision of race relations and gender issues..." In fact, the way in which Barton managed the Galveston crisis proved to be her undoing, for the American Red Cross was becoming too large and formalized to continue to do business in the personal, charm-based manner Barton preferred.

By the time Barton turned 83, those in charge agreed that it was time for her to resign. Much to her chagrin, the woman who had advanced the cause of her gender with such fervor was replaced by an entirely male leadership. Not to be completely left behind, Barton soon founded the National First Aid Society and devoted the remainder of her life to promoting its ideals and programs. Working out of her home in Glen Echo, Maryland, she also completed her final book, the autobiographical *The Story of My Childhood*, in 1907. She lived to see her 90th birthday before dying on April 12, 1912 from pneumonia.

Barton had lived a long and fulfilling life, but her legacy has extended even further, and it continues to be felt across the nation she so faithfully served over 100 years after her death.

Barton's last house

A photograph of Barton with the red cross

A 1948 commemorative stamp honoring Barton

Online Resources

Other books about 19th century American history by Charles River Editors

Other books about Civil War history by Charles River Editors

Other books about Clara Barton on Amazon

Further Reading

Barton, William E. The Life of Clara Barton Founder of the American Red Cross. (1922).

Burton, David Henry. Clara Barton: in the service of humanity (Greenwood, 1995)

Crompton, Samuel Etinde. Clara Barton: Humanitarian. New York: Chelsea House, 2009.

Deady, Kathleen W. Clara Barton. Mankato: Capstone Press, 2003.

Dulles Foster R. The American Red Cross: A History (1950)

Oates, Stephen B. A Woman of Valor: Clara Barton and the Civil War. New York: Free Press, 1994.

Pryor, Elizabeth Brown. Clara Barton: Professional Angel. Philadelphia: University of Pennsylvania Press, 1987

Ross, Ishbel. Angel of the Battlefield: The Life of Clara Barton. New York: Harper and Brothers Publishers, 1956.

Free Books by Charles River Editors

We have brand new titles available for free most days of the week. To see which of our titles are currently free, click on this link.

Discounted Books by Charles River Editors

We have titles at a discount price of just 99 cents everyday. To see which of our titles are currently 99 cents, click on this link.

Made in United States
Orlando, FL
07 September 2022